The Life and World of

ELIZABETH I

Struan Reid

First published in Great Britain by Heinemann Library, Halley Court, Jordan Hill, Oxford OX2 8EJ, part of Harcourt Education. Heinemann is a registered trademark of Harcourt Education Ltd.

Editorial: Lucy Thunder and Helen Cox
Design: Ron Kamen and Celia Floyd
Illustrations: Jeff Edwards and Joanna Brooker
Picture Research: Rebecca Sodergren and Elaine Willis
Production: Séverine Ribierre

Originated by Ambassador Litho Ltd
Printed in Hong Kong, China
by Wing King Tong

ISBN 0 431 14781 7
07 06 05 04 03
10 9 8 7 6 5 4 3 2 1

British Library Cataloguing in Publication Data
Reid, Struan
Life and world of Elizabeth I
942'.055'02

A full catalogue record for this book is available from the British Library.

Acknowledgements

The Publishers would like to thank the following for permission to reproduce photographs:
Bridgeman Art Library/Trustees of the National Museums & Galleries on Merseyside p. **4**; Bridgeman Art Library/Thyssen-Nomemisza Collection, Madrid, Spain p. **6**; Bridgeman Art Library/Hever Castle Ltd, Kent p. **7**; Bridgeman Art Library/Mark Fiennes, Loseley Park, Surrey p. **10**; Bridgeman Art Library/Prado Madrid, Spain p. **11**; Bridgeman Art Library/Hatfield House, Hertfordshire p. **12**; Bridgeman Art Library/National Portrait Gallery, London p. **13**; Bridgeman Art Library/Burghley House Collection, Lincolnshire p. **14**; Bridgeman Art Library/British Museum p. **15**; Bridgeman Art Library/Hermitage, St Petersburg p. **16**; Bridgeman Art Library/Mark Fiennes, Wollaton Hall, Nottingham p. **19**; Bridgeman Art Library/Scottish NAtional Portrait Gallery, Edinburgh p. **20**; Bridgeman Art Library/Castle Museum and Art Gallery, Nottingham p. **21**; Bridgeman Art Library/Victoria and Albert Museum p. **22**; Bridgeman Art Library/Society of Apothecaries, London p. **23**; Bridgeman Art Library/The Stapleton Collection p. **25**; Bridgeman Art Library/British Library p. **26**; Bridgeman Art Library/Fitzwilliam Museum, University of Cambridge p. **28**; Bridgeman Art Library/Private Collection p. **4**; Bridgeman Art Library/Roy Miles Fine Paintings p. **29**; British Library p. **24**; Hulton Getty p. **9**; Penhurst Place p. **17**; The Royal Collection © HM Queen Elizabeth II p. **8**; Topham Picturepoint p. **27**.

Cover photograph of Elizabeth I, reproduced with permission of the National Portrait Gallery.

The Publishers would like to thank Rebecca Vickers for her assistance in the preparation of this book.

Every effort has been made to contact copyright holders of any material reproduced in this book. Any omissions will be rectified in subsequent printings if notice is given to the Publishers.

Disclaimer

Contents

Any words appearing in the text in bold, **like this**, are explained in the Glossary.

Who was Queen Elizabeth?

Elizabeth I was a brilliant and powerful queen who ruled England over 400 years ago. When she came to the throne in 1558, she **inherited** a deeply divided kingdom. For many years the people of England had been fighting each other over matters of religion. Queen Elizabeth was an extremely clever ruler and, by the time of her death nearly 50 years later, she had managed to unite her people. By then England had become one of the richest and most powerful countries in Europe.

A strong female ruler

Many people think that Elizabeth was the greatest English **monarch** who has ever reigned. She was the second daughter of King Henry VIII and the last member of the **Tudors**. The Tudor family was a royal **dynasty** that ruled England for more than a hundred years.

Elizabeth ruled her country at a time when most of the world's leaders were men, but she was as cunning and as quick as the best of them. She was much loved by her people and became known affectionately as Good Queen Bess.

▲ When she became queen, Elizabeth was always painted wearing the most magnificent clothes and jewels. In this way she showed herself to be a strong and powerful ruler.

How do we know?

We know a lot about Elizabeth I. Many portraits were painted of her and poems were written about her. Plays and music were composed for her by some of the most talented people of the day. These and many other sources, such as letters and government records, provide us with detailed information about the life and times of Elizabeth I – what she looked like and how she lived.

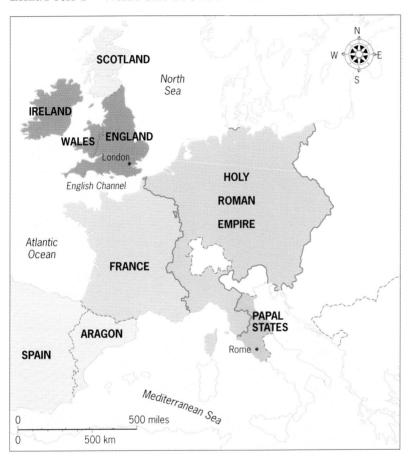

◄ This map shows the main kingdoms of Europe at the time Elizabeth I was born.

Key dates

1533   Henry VIII marries Anne Boleyn; Princess Elizabeth is born

1547   Henry VIII dies and Edward VI **succeeds** him

1553   Edward VI dies; Princess Mary becomes Queen Mary I

1558   Elizabeth becomes Queen of England when Mary I dies

1570   Elizabeth is **excommunicated** by the Pope

1588   The Spanish **Armada** is defeated

1603   Queen Elizabeth I dies

The birth of a princess

Elizabeth's father was King Henry VIII. He had already been ruling England for 24 years by the time Elizabeth was born. He was first married to a Spanish princess called Catherine of Aragon. She had given birth to a daughter, called Mary. At this time it was believed that kings were always much stronger and commanded more respect than queens. Henry longed to have a son who could **succeed** him, but Queen Catherine was now too old to have any more children.

A new wife

By now, Henry had fallen in love with a beautiful young lady at the royal court, called Anne Boleyn. He wanted to marry her and hoped that she would be able to give him the son he longed for. However, the Pope would not allow him to end his marriage to Catherine, so Henry decided to break with the **Catholic** Church in Rome. In 1534, he declared that he was now head of the Church in England. This meant he was now free to marry Anne. Although Henry refused to obey the Pope, he still kept his Catholic faith and did not become a **Protestant**.

▲ This portrait of Elizabeth's father, King Henry VIII, was painted by a famous German artist, called Hans Holbein. The king was proud of his looks and was a very good sportsman and musician as well as being a powerful king.

On 7 September 1533, at Greenwich Palace, the new Queen Anne gave birth to a princess, who was named Elizabeth. Henry was disappointed as he still had no son. The baby princess was born at one of the most important and exciting times in European history, when there were great religious upheavals that would change the world forever.

▶ Anne Boleyn, Elizabeth's mother. When she was a girl, Anne was sent away to be educated in France, where she learned to dress and behave in an elegant way. When she returned to England, she quickly caught the eye of King Henry VIII.

The Reformation

At this time, the Pope was head of the Roman Catholic Church and everyone, including kings, was supposed to obey everything he said. In 1517, a movement called the Reformation began. Some priests, such as Martin Luther, tried to reform or change certain things within the Roman Catholic Church. Their protests ended with the Christian Church splitting in two, with Catholics on one side and Protestants on the other. Roman Catholicism was eventually replaced in some countries by a new, reformed religion known as Protestantism.

A lonely childhood

Princess Elizabeth grew up away from the royal court. She saw very little of her parents and was looked after by nannies and nurses. Elizabeth was brought up as a **Protestant**. When aged only four, she began learning about **astronomy**, mathematics, history and geography. She also learned French and Italian. She was an extremely intelligent girl and read as many books as she could. Later, she learned Greek and Latin from her tutor. She could play musical instruments like the **virginals** and a guitar-like instrument called the lute. Elizabeth was also a very good dancer.

Terror at court

Princess Elizabeth's mother, Anne Boleyn, was in great danger. She had still not given birth to a baby boy and King Henry was beginning to spend more of his time with a lady-in-waiting called Jane Seymour.

▼ A portrait of Elizabeth aged 13. She is shown with books, and was one of the most educated women of her day.

Henry started plotting against Queen Anne. She was accused of all sorts of terrible crimes, including having love affairs with other men behind the king's back. On 19 May 1536, Anne was **executed** at the Tower of London. Elizabeth, who was less than three years old when her mother died, probably did not really know what had happened. She was still so young and had seen so little of her mother ever since she was born.

Elizabeth's stepmothers

A few days after Anne Boleyn's execution, King Henry married Jane Seymour and both Elizabeth and her half-sister Mary were declared **illegitimate**. This was a very dangerous time for the two princesses and Elizabeth soon learned to keep quiet so as not to attract attention.

In 1537, Jane Seymour gave birth to the longed-for son and heir, who was named Edward, but she died soon afterwards. Henry married three more times and so Elizabeth had three more stepmothers: Anne of Cleves, whom Henry just as quickly divorced; Catherine Howard, who, like her cousin Anne Boleyn, was executed; and finally Catherine Parr, who managed to outlive the king.

▲ This engraving shows Elizabeth being taught by her tutor Roger Ascham (1515–68). He was a brilliant scholar who encouraged the young princess in her learning.

The ordinary people

Most ordinary people in Tudor times lived completely different lives from the luxurious sort enjoyed by the **courtiers** surrounding the king. They lived in small, isolated villages in the countryside, far away from large cities like London. Most worked as farmers or labourers in the fields. Many were very poor and had little to eat. Mothers often died in childbirth and many children died from terrible diseases. It was a difficult time to be poor.

Living in fear

While Henry was married to his last wife, Catherine Parr, Elizabeth and Mary spent more time at the royal court. Catherine was very fond of Elizabeth. The princesses saw more of their little half-brother, Edward, and Elizabeth was with him when their father died in 1547.

The boy king

Edward then **succeeded** his father as Edward VI. He was only nine years old when he became king. Like his half-sister Elizabeth he had been brought up as a **Protestant** and so, for as long as Edward was on the throne, Elizabeth was safe. Unfortunately the new king had always been a sickly child and he died on 6 July 1553, aged fifteen.

A divided kingdom

England was thrown into chaos as Protestants and **Catholics** fought each other for control. Catholic Mary eventually won the support of most of the people of England and was crowned queen. She recognized the Pope as head of the Church in England and restored Catholicism as the state religion. In 1554 she married her Catholic cousin, Prince Philip of Spain.

▶ Edward VI was very well-educated, but he was still a boy when he came to the throne. During his short reign of only six years, England was really ruled by his uncle, the Duke of Somerset.

Princess in the Tower

In February 1554, there was a plot to place Elizabeth on the throne instead of Mary. This was discovered and defeated. Elizabeth was sent to prison in the Tower of London, even though it could not be proved that she had supported the **rebellion**. She remained in prison for three months until she was released in May. But Queen Mary still did not trust her and thought that she was too dangerous to be left alone.

Queen Mary believed she could force the Protestants of England to become Catholic again, and from 1555 nearly 300 Protestants were burned at the stake. Mary was also desperate for a child so that she would be succeeded on the throne by a Catholic. Protestant Elizabeth was still the next in line to be queen. Twice Mary believed that she was pregnant, but she never did have a baby.

▲ Queen Mary was 17 years older than her half-sister Elizabeth. She always felt that it was her duty to reverse many of the changes that their father, King Henry VIII, had introduced.

A Protestant rebellion

In February 1554, a Protestant called Sir Thomas Wyatt led un uprising of 3000 men against Queen Mary. They planned to overthrow Mary and place Elizabeth on the English throne instead. The **rebels** believed that Mary's planned marriage to Prince Philip of Spain would lead to England becoming part of the Catholic Spanish Empire. The rebellion failed and all the leaders were **executed**.

Elizabeth the queen

On 17 November 1558, Mary died and Elizabeth succeeded her as Queen of England. Elizabeth was 25 years old. She was crowned queen at Westminster Abbey in London on 15 January 1559. Elizabeth was now the ruler of a country deeply divided between **Catholics** and **Protestants**. Many of the Catholics, especially the Church leaders who had been chosen by Mary, did not recognize Elizabeth as queen. Even the Protestants argued amongst themselves about the sort of Church they wanted.

England in danger

England was also a weak country when Elizabeth came to the throne. It had very little money and it was threatened by much more powerful Catholic countries to the south, especially France and Spain. The fact that Elizabeth was a woman made her position even weaker. This was a time when most rulers were men. Any countries ruled by women were considered to be weak and, therefore, open to attack from abroad and even from inside the country itself.

▲ Hatfield Old Palace in Hertfordshire. Elizabeth was being kept prisoner here when she heard the news that Mary had died and that she was now Queen of England.

A majestic queen

One of Elizabeth's **courtiers** described her in this way: 'Slender and straight; ... her countenance [face] was somewhat long, but yet of admirable beauty, in a most delightful composition of majesty and modesty.'

Elizabeth was about 1.62 m tall and had brown eyes and curly golden red hair with a fair complexion. When she was a princess, she dressed simply with very little jewellery, as she did not want to draw attention to herself. When she became queen she dressed in magnificent clothes made from silks, velvets and furs, and wore fantastic jewels. She dressed to impress her people and foreign **ambassadors**.

▲ This portrait shows Elizabeth in her coronation robes. She is pictured wearing the crown of England on her head and holding the orb and sceptre, symbols of royal power, in her hands.

Clothes for show and for work

The men and women who attended Elizabeth I at her royal court were expected to spend a fortune on their clothes. They were made from the most expensive materials available, like velvet, silk, fur and lace. They were also adorned with beautiful gold jewellery. But most ordinary people in **Tudor** times made their own clothes at home from cotton and wool. Their clothes had to be tough so that they could last a long time.

Loyal advisers

When Elizabeth was growing up, she was never given instruction on how to rule or govern a country. As a girl she was not expected to become ruler of England. But the dangerous times she lived through taught her how to survive and who to trust. When she became Queen of England, Elizabeth liked the taste of power and she made it clear that she would be in charge.

Helpful advice

Elizabeth I was what is known as an absolute ruler. She made all the final decisions on how the country was governed. She could not do everything herself, however, and so she had help from members of her Privy Council. This was a group of men who acted as her advisers.

One of the closest and most important advisers was William Cecil, Lord Burghley. He was Elizabeth's Principal Secretary and he advised her on how to spend the country's money and on England's contacts with other countries. For the next 40 years he would guide the queen through many dangerous situations.

◄ Lord Burghley (1520–98) rose to become one of the most powerful men in the land and was one of Elizabeth's most respected advisers.

▲ Nonsuch Palace, painted by George Hoefnagel in 1582. Lying to the south-west of London in Surrey, the palace was built by Henry VIII. It was one of Elizabeth's favourite homes and she liked to go hunting in its park.

A new Church

The most important and difficult matter that Elizabeth faced when she came to the throne was that of religion. She made **Protestantism** the official religion of the country. She tried to lead the people of England towards a religion that lay between the beliefs of the **Puritans** on one side, who had been backed by Edward VI, and the **Roman Catholics** on the other, who had been backed by Queen Mary.

Elizabeth hoped that most people in the country would join her Church, so that they could finally settle down and stop fighting each other. Many did, but others refused to recognize her or her Church and so they were hunted down and either **executed** or had to leave the country.

A network of spies

Another of Elizabeth's loyal advisers was called Sir Francis Walsingham (c. 1532–1590). As Secretary of State, he set up a huge network of spies that spread throughout England and across the sea to France, Italy and Spain. Elizabeth always lived in fear of attack. Walsingham's spies sent him information on any planned **rebellions** against the queen. They also protected Elizabeth from plots to kill her.

Married to her country

When Elizabeth became queen, her advisers and all the people of England expected her to marry. In those days they believed that a woman would need the help of a husband to rule the country. They also feared that there would be a **civil war** if Elizabeth did not have a child, who would be the obvious ruler after her death.

During her marriage talks with foreign princes, Elizabeth played one off against the other, holding out the possibility to each of them that they might be able to catch her. In this way, Elizabeth used herself as a source of strength to win more **allies** and power.

A long list of suitors

There were many European princes who were eager to marry the queen. Elizabeth was one of the most desirable women in Europe. One of the first to propose marriage to her was King Philip II of Spain. He had already been married to Elizabeth's half-sister Queen Mary. But he was a **Catholic** and his marriage to Mary had been very unpopular in England. Elizabeth did not want to make the same mistake, so she turned down his offer.

▶ Francis, Duke of Alençon (1554–84). Although he was a Catholic prince, he opposed the strong anti-protestant policies of his brother, King Charles IX of France.

Elizabeth began thinking that it would be safer if she married an Englishman. One man who had known Elizabeth all her life was Robert Dudley, Earl of Leicester. He was already married, however. When his wife was killed falling down some stairs, people began whispering that Robert had had her murdered so that he could marry the queen. These rumours were probably untrue, but they made it impossible for Elizabeth to marry him.

▲ This painting shows Elizabeth dancing with Robert Dudley, one of her favourite courtiers. She was a very good dancer and musician, and loved to relax in this way with her friends.

A strong contender

One man who came very close to marrying Elizabeth was Francis, Duke of Alençon. He was the brother of the King of France, but he was another Catholic prince and Elizabeth's advisers thought that it would be too risky to have a Catholic married to their **Protestant** queen. In the end, Elizabeth never married and never had any children. She would later say that she was married to England.

Royal marriages

Royal marriages, like the one between Mary and Philip II of Spain, were extremely important in **Tudor** times. They were regarded as the best way in which to make powerful **alliances** between countries. The rulers of smaller countries would always try to marry their royal children to the sons and daughters of the rulers of more powerful countries. In this way they hoped to strengthen their position and protect themselves from attack by other countries.

A dazzling court

Elizabeth attracted a huge circle of **courtiers** around her. As well as her advisers, there were friends and other people who entertained her. Some hoped to win her favour to help them up the ladder to positions of power. Adventurers and explorers, such as Sir Francis Drake and Sir Walter Raleigh, wanted to win her backing for their **expeditions**. A small army of ladies-in-waiting went everywhere with the queen, looking after her comfort and her magnificent clothes and jewels.

▲ The queen was like the sun shining at the centre of her court. Whenever she went out in public, she dazzled everyone who saw her.

Work and play

Much of Elizabeth's day was spent at her royal duties, meeting her advisers and foreign **ambassadors**. When her working day was over, Elizabeth sat with her friends and ladies-in-waiting to listen to music, dance, play cards and read poetry. She enjoyed watching plays, too, and writers such as Ben Jonson and, later, William Shakespeare wrote plays and poems for her. Artists visited the court to paint magnificent portraits of her. Elizabeth loved sports and was very good at riding, tennis and archery.

▲ This is a modern photograph of Wollaton Hall in Nottinghamshire, which was built in the 1580s by one of Elizabeth's courtiers, Sir Francis Willoughby. The queen often stayed at the houses of her courtiers during her annual 'progress', and she expected to be entertained on a royal scale.

The royal progress

Elizabeth inherited nearly 60 royal residences when she came to the throne. Once a year, during the summer months, Elizabeth and all her **court** would 'progress' from one palace to another. It was very important for Elizabeth to show herself to her people. In this way they were reminded of her presence and power. The queen herself, dressed in splendid clothes, travelled in a coach with open sides so that she could be seen and admired.

Exploring the world

During the 15th and 16th centuries, European seafarers, like Christopher Columbus, began to explore the world. Until then, Europeans knew very little about other countries beyond their shores. In 1577, Sir Francis Drake set out from England and sailed all the way round the world on his ship, the *Golden Hind*. Other English explorers, like Humphrey Gilbert and Sir Walter Raleigh, established settlements in North America.

Royal cousins

In 1568, Elizabeth had to face one of the greatest dangers of her entire reign. In that year her cousin, Queen Mary of Scotland, fled south across the border into England. She had been imprisoned by Scottish **rebels** and forced to give up the Scottish crown to her small son. Only thirteen months old, he now became King James VI of Scotland. Mary begged Elizabeth to help her.

A difficult dilemma

Elizabeth was very suspicious of her cousin. Mary was a **Catholic** and there were many people, both in England and abroad, who believed that she should really be Queen of England instead of Elizabeth. They thought that Henry VIII's marriage to Elizabeth's mother, Anne Boleyn, had not been legal. Mary was allowed to stay in England, but while she lived in great comfort at Elizabeth's expense, she was really under arrest and she was to remain under guard for the next nineteen years.

◄ Mary Queen of Scots was nine years younger than her cousin Elizabeth. She became Queen of Scotland when she was only six days old. Mary was very beautiful, but not a very good ruler.

The kingdom in the north

Scotland had always been a separate kingdom from England. Since 1371 it had been ruled by a royal **dynasty** called the Stuarts. Scotland and England had fought many battles against each other, but there had also been marriage **alliances** between the two countries. King James IV of Scotland married Princess Margaret of England, the sister of Henry VIII. Their granddaughter was Mary Queen of Scots.

Mary is executed

In 1570 the Pope **excommunicated** Elizabeth, giving all English Catholics the right to disobey and rebel against her. A number of plots against Elizabeth were uncovered over the following years and their leaders **executed**. Her advisers warned her that she was in great danger and that Mary must be executed, but she refused to kill her cousin and fellow queen.

Finally, in 1586, it was proved beyond doubt that Mary was plotting against Elizabeth. Letters written to Mary from a young Catholic called Anthony Babington were intercepted by Walsingham's spies. Mary's replies proved that she supported Babington's plan to murder Elizabeth.

Mary was sent for trial and, on 8 February 1587, she was executed. She was 44 years old when she died and had spent nearly half her life as a prisoner of Elizabeth, but the two queens had never met one another.

▲ This 19th century painting shows Mary Queen of Scots being led to her execution at Fotheringay Castle in Northamptonshire. When her son James **succeeded** Elizabeth as King of England, he had the castle pulled down.

Attack from Spain

When Mary Queen of Scots was **executed**, all the ports round England were closed to delay the news reaching Europe. When the **Catholic** rulers of Europe finally heard of her death, they were horrified. King Philip II of Spain now decided that it was his duty to attack Elizabeth and claim the crown of England for himself.

The Spanish Armada

King Philip was a very proud man. He had never forgotten nor forgiven Elizabeth for refusing his offer of marriage. He also knew that she had been sending money and soldiers to help his **Protestant** enemies in his lands in the Netherlands. In 1588, Philip put together an enormous fleet of 130 ships to attack England. It was known as the **Armada**. On 19 July, the fleet was sighted off the south-west coast of England. The Spanish ships sailed up the Channel, followed by the English.

When the Armada anchored off the coast of northern France, the English sent in fire boats to force them out into the open seas. The Spanish sailed out in great confusion and the English gave chase.

The Armada was finally driven north and away from England. Battered by winds and driving rain, the ships were blown all the way round England, Scotland and past Ireland. Many were wrecked along the way. Only half of the original 130 ships made it back to the safety of Spain.

◀ The Armada Jewel was made for Elizabeth to celebrate the defeat of the Spanish Armada. It is made of gold and brightly coloured enamels, and contains a portrait of the queen.

Elizabeth's reaction

Before the arrival of the Spanish Armada off the coast of England, Elizabeth travelled to Tilbury on the River Thames. Here she gave a famous speech to inspire her soldiers and sailors. The speech showed Elizabeth as a strong leader, who was not afraid of the Spanish, or anything or anyone else.

▲ This painting shows English ships fighting the Spanish Armada. The Spanish ships were huge, lumbering monsters, much better suited to defending than attacking.

Battleships

England and Spain had about the same number of ships when they fought each other in 1588. But the ships on the two sides were very different. The Spanish ships were enormous and difficult to steer in cramped areas. They carried huge cannons made of brass and iron that fired heavy cannon balls. The English ships were smaller and lighter so they were much quicker and more nimble in the water. They carried much lighter cannons that could be fired more often. Their crews were also more experienced than the Spanish.

The final years

The defeat of the Spanish **Armada** was celebrated throughout the land and Elizabeth I's popularity soared among her people. She came to symbolize the success and glory of her country. England had defeated an attack from the most powerful country in Europe. Now, 30 years after she had first come to the throne, Elizabeth could feel sure of her position as queen of a strong and united **Protestant** country.

Changing times

As the years passed and Elizabeth grew older, however, things began to change. Even though the Armada had been defeated, the war with Spain continued to drag on. This fighting was very expensive and **taxes** had to be raised in order to pay for the war. Although the people of England still loved their queen, they started to complain about having to pay more and more for the fighting. From 1594 there were four years of bad harvests and many people had little food and were going hungry.

◀ This engraving shows Queen Elizabeth on her throne, with her Privy Counsellors. They were her servants as well as her advisers.

New faces

Elizabeth's close friends and advisers were growing old and dying. One of the first to go was Lord Leicester, who had known Elizabeth since she was a girl. Sir Christopher Hatton, one of her favourite **courtiers** and her **Lord Chancellor**, and the loyal Sir Francis Walsingham died in the next few years. Lord Burghley was growing old and tired.

New men, such as Burghley's son Robert Cecil, were beginning to take over the important positions of power in the land. As Elizabeth's reign drew to a close and the expensive war with Spain dragged on, the members of **Parliament** began to question her authority and her requests for more money. This would have been unimaginable at the beginning of her reign. Elizabeth was beginning to feel isolated and alone.

▲ Robert Cecil, Earl of Salisbury, was the second son of Lord Burghley and **succeeded** his father as chief adviser to Elizabeth and, later, King James VI and I.

God's creation

Europeans in **Tudor** times believed in the idea that God created everything in a strict **hierarchy**, or chain. This was known as the Chain of Being and stretched down from God, through the angels, humans and down to the lowliest things like animals and plants. Some humans, like kings and queens, were seen as higher than others in the chain. **Monarchs** at that time believed that they were appointed by God to rule. This 'divine right of kings' gave them enormous power and influence and their word became law. Parliament was used to pass laws and raise taxes whenever they were demanded by the monarch.

The death of a great queen

As well as losing old friends and advisers, in her old age Elizabeth was losing her looks. She still took immense care over her appearance and wore magnificent clothes and jewels, but her golden red hair was now thin and grey and she wore a wig to cover it up. Her drawn and wrinkled face was covered with white makeup and powder. She became tired very easily and she suffered from painful toothache.

A disloyal courtier

Elizabeth was hit by a bitter blow in her final years. One of her **courtiers**, called the Earl of Essex, returned to England in disgrace after leading a disastrous military **expedition** to Ireland. In desperation and fearing he would be thrown into prison, he tried to raise a **rebellion** against the queen. He was arrested and, in 1601, he was **executed**. Elizabeth was very sorry to sign his **death warrant** as she had known him since he was a boy and had been very fond of him, but she had no choice.

▲ A painting of Queen Elizabeth's funeral procession. Her coffin was drawn through the streets of London, accompanied by some of the most important people in the land.

◄ Queen Elizabeth's tomb at Westminster Abbey. Her successor, King James, erected this large white marble monument to her memory in 1606.

The royal succession

Throughout her long reign, Elizabeth had always refused to name the person she wanted to rule England after her. Now, as that time approached, she still kept everyone guessing to the very end. Early in 1603, Elizabeth caught a chill and moved to her favourite palace at Richmond to recover. By March she had grown so ill that she could eat very little. She grew weaker and weaker and, in the early hours of 24 March 1603, Elizabeth I, the last of the **Tudors**, died peacefully in her sleep. She was 69 and had reigned for 44 years.

A messenger was sent from Richmond to carry the news to King James VI of Scotland. The son of Elizabeth's cousin and old enemy, Mary Queen of Scots, had now become James I of England.

London in Elizabeth's time

By the time of Elizabeth's death in 1603, London had grown into one of the largest and most important cities in Europe. Many thousands of people lived there. Rich nobles and **merchants** lived in grand mansions, but most people were packed into tall, narrow houses and lived in cramp conditions. There was a busy port and ships sailed up and down the River Thames, which ran through the middle of the city.

The end of a golden age

Elizabeth I's body was taken from Richmond by boat to her palace in Whitehall, London. Her funeral was held in Westminster Abbey at the end of April, and as the **procession** wound its way through the streets of London there was 'a general sighing, groaning and weeping' among the crowds that lined the streets. Elizabeth I was buried in a magnificent tomb next to that of her half-sister, Mary. In another chamber nearby lies the body of Mary Queen of Scots. In death, Elizabeth was finally united with the two Marys who had played such an important part in her life.

England mourns

Many people throughout England **mourned** Elizabeth's death. They saw her long reign as a golden age in England's history. They forgot about how difficult their lives had been in the final years, the shortages of food and the constant demands for money to pay for expensive wars. They preferred to remember Elizabeth as a wise and loving queen who protected her country and her people from many threats and dangers.

▶ This miniature portrait of Queen Elizabeth by the famous artist Nicholas Hilliard is shown here bigger than it really is. Even in old age, the queen was still portayed in splendid clothes and jewels.

Elizabeth did make mistakes, especially at the start of her reign. She had received no training in how to govern a country and she was given bad advice by some of her advisers. After these early mistakes Elizabeth made it clear that she would be the one in charge. She often found it difficult to make up her mind on important matters. Once she did, however, she did it with a determination and certainty that impressed her friends and her enemies, too.

◀ This is a portrait of King James VI of Scotland, James I of England. As soon as he was told of Elizabeth's death, he hurried south to London to claim his new throne.

A sense of pride

When Elizabeth died, she left England a proud, confident and strong nation. She united her people under the **Protestant** faith and they looked out as equal partners with the other nations of Europe. Her reign is of such importance in the history of England that she was the first English ruler to give her name to an age. The Elizabethan age was truly a golden era.

Glossary

alliance being united, through a formal treaty or an agreement, such as a marriage

allies two or more people or countries united by some formal agreement

ambassador person who represents the interests of their own country in another country

Armada large number of ships, from the Spanish word for 'great fleet'

astronomy scientific study of the stars and planets

Catholic member of the Christian Roman Catholic Church, headed by the Pope in Rome

civil war war fought between two sides within the same country

court home of a king and queen and their household and followers

courtier attendant at a royal court

death warrant document that, when signed, allows someone to be put to death

dynasty series of rulers belonging to the same family

excommunicate cast someone out of membership of the Church, particularly the Catholic Church

execute put someone to death

expedition organized journey or voyage, for exploration, military or scientific purposes

hierarchy system of arranging people or things in a graded order, from top to bottom

illegitimate someone who was born when their parents were not legally married to each other

inherit receive property or a title from someone who has died

Lord Chancellor chief adviser to the English monarch

merchant someone who trades with other countries, buying and selling different goods

monarch king, queen, emperor or empress who rules a country

mourn to express sadness at the death or loss of someone

Parliament body that passes the laws of the land and raises taxes. In Elizabeth I's time, Parliament had less power than it does today.

procession group of people moving forward in an organized, ceremonial way

Protestant member of the Protestant branch of the Christian Church, which broke away from the Catholic Church, headed by the Pope

Puritan extreme Protestant who wants to purify the Church of England

rebel someone who resists or rises up against a government or ruler

rebellion organized resistance to a government or ruler

succeed to follow as the new king or queen

taxes money that individuals have to pay to the government

Tudor royal dynasty that ruled England from 1485 until 1603

virginals early form of the piano, in which the strings are plucked rather than struck

Timeline

1509   Henry VIII becomes King of England. Henry marries Princess Catherine of Aragon.

1516   Princess Mary is born

1517   The beginning of the Reformation in Europe (Protestantism)

1533   Henry divorces Catherine of Aragon and marries Anne Boleyn. Princess Elizabeth is born.

1534   Henry declares himself head of the Church in England

1536   Queen Anne Boleyn is executed. Henry marries Jane Seymour.

1537   Prince Edward is born

1542   Princess Mary of Scotland is born. She becomes queen six days later when her father, James V, dies.

1547   Edward becomes King of England when Henry VIII dies

1553   Edward VI dies and is succeeded by his half-sister Mary

1558   Mary I dies and Elizabeth I succeeds her

1568   Mary Queen of Scots escapes to England

1570   Pope excommunicates Elizabeth I

1587   Mary Queen of Scots is executed

1588   The Spanish Armada is defeated

1603   Elizabeth I dies and James VI (James I) becomes King of England as well as King of Scotland

Further reading & websites

Investigating the Tudors, A. Honey (National Trust, 1993)

Queen Elizabeth I, R. Bell (Heinemann Library, 1999)

Queen Elizabeth I, P. Burns (Wayland, 1999)

Heinemann Explore – an online resource from Heinemann.
For Key Stage 2 history go to *www.heinemannexplore.co.uk*
www.elizabethi.org/
http://tudorhistory.org/elizabeth/

Places to visit

Hatfield House, Hertfordshire   Burghley House, Northamptonshire

Westminster Abbey, London   Tower of London

Index

Titles in the *Life and World Of* series include:

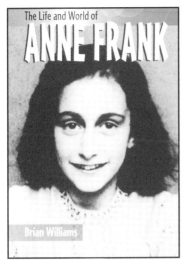

Hardback   0 431 14780 9

Hardback   0 431 14781 7

Hardback   0 431 14782 5

Hardback   0 431 14783 3

Hardback   0 431 14784 1

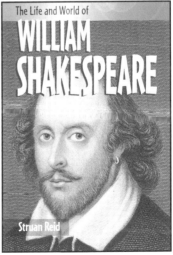

Hardback   0 431 14785 X

Find out about the other titles in this series on our website www.heinemann.co.uk/library